EVERYDAY
Daily Routine Workbook

Daily Routine Workbook
© 2021 PB Terry-Smith, Ph.D., Th.D.
www.coachpositive.com
www.drpterrysmith.com

ISBN: 978-0-9885429-8-3

Table of Contents

INTRODUCTION

You have already read our Routine report, so I don't want to beat you over the head with info about how powerful creating (or adjusting) routines can be to your life.

This companion Workbook will take the info from the book, and put it into a format that will allow you to take action right now!

So what are we waiting for? Let's get started...

Change is inevitable.

Whether it is on a macro level like the world, or a micro level like your own bubble – change cannot be stopped.

Instead of fearing change, you should embrace it. When the world around you changes, it is a chance for you to capitalize and change with the times. When your life changes, it's a fresh start.

If you struggle with change, then you are in the right place.

In this workbook you will:

- Learn if it's time to change
- Figure out what you want to change
- Create goals that help you change

If you are ready to **pivot** towards more success, happiness and fulfillment then keep reading!

FIGURE OUT YOUR WHY

Before you begin to look at your daily tasks and routines, you need to first think about what you really want to accomplish. The easiest way to do this, is to examine (or set) some long term goals.

For maximum effect, you should choose one or two goals that address multiple areas of your life.

Work Goals	
Family Goals	
Health Goals	
Spiritual Goals	
Financial Goals	
Household Goals	

EXAMINE YOUR DAY

Now that you have some goals, you will have a general idea of what you want your newly created routines to eventually accomplish.

Before we start working on routines though, we need to examine our current day and the things we are already doing. To start examining your day, simply spend a day recording all the tasks you do. Start with a single day, but keep in mind recording a whole week will be significantly more helpful.

Start recording things like:

- Think about the things you have to do before you go to work
- Think about everything you need to do to help your family get their day started
- Consider the repeatable tasks you need to do at work
- Consider the repeatable tasks you need to do to keep the household running (cleaning, organizing, eating, etc...)
- Ask yourself what errands you need to complete
- Ask yourself what things you do to stay in good health
- Think about the things you do for your financial health

We leave some space below for you to record, but feel free to use your own notebook.

My Daily Tasks

EXAMINE YOUR LIST

Now that you have your list, examine it and take stock of the things you do daily. Ask yourself the following questions about each task...

Are My Tasks Positive or Negative?	
Positive Tasks I Do Daily	**Negative Tasks I Do Daily**

What Tasks Progress Me Towards My Goals?

What Tasks Are an Efficient Use of My Time?

If you find a number of daily tasks that are positive, fit your goals and efficient uses of your time – highlight them.

These are powerful daily routines that you already have and you should commit to continuing and perfecting them.

Alternatively, if tasks don't tick off all the 3 above boxes, you might want to look at dropping them, or replacing them with new routines.

LOOK FOR WEAKNESS

Compare your goals from earlier to your list of daily tasks and ask yourself:

Are any of your goals not being addressed properly?

List any goals that you don't think aren't being addressed:

These are the goals/areas that you should focus creating new routines to address.

BRAINSTORM NEW ROUTINES

Using the list from above, think of 2-3 simple things you could do each day that address the areas of life you feel are lacking.

POTENTIAL NEW ROUTINES	
Goals/Areas in my Life Lacking	Routines to Address Them

SCHEDULE YOUR NEW ROUTINES

Ideally after the last step, you will have a number of potential new routines you can start to incorporate into your life.

You should take some time now, to figure out how these will best fit into your life.

If you are someone who already has a day planner, and you schedule your life down to the hour – then you will simply plot these new routines where they fit.

We aren't including a calendar here, as there are many apps, programs, templates and websites that can do a much better job than that.

To start though, simply slot your new routines into three categories. Think about where your new routines best fit into your current schedule so you aren't trying to fit round pegs into square holes.

MORNING ROUTINES	AFTERNOON ROUTINES	NIGHT ROUTINES

STICK TO THEM

Committing to doing a new daily task, no matter how trivial, isn't just as simple as wanting to do it. If that were the case, we would all get enough exercise, save a ton of money and have a totally clean and organized house.

The truth is, committing to a new routine is much tougher than simply creating one.

To help your routine stick you should take a couple of steps:

1. **Commit to 30 Days**

2. **Use a Calendar or App to Mark Each Day Done** - There is something really powerful about seeing your progress right in front of you.

3. **Build in Flexibility** – Don't beat yourself up over missing a day

4. **Build in a Reward -** You should try and think of a reward that you can give yourself if you go the full 30 days with your new routine(s).

POTENTIAL REWARDS IF YOU LAST 30 DAYS

REFLECT & RETARGET

Once you have reached the end of your month (ideally successfully) it is time to sit back and take some time to reflect on how it went. Ask yourself these questions:

What went well with my new routine?

Did my new routine have an appreciable effect on my life?

What part of my new routine did I struggle with?

What part of my routine did I truly enjoy?

What could I do to make my routine more efficient?

Is this something I want to continue?

Is there a better use of my time?

Wrap Up

It's a routine right? You don't stop doing it. Take what you learned from the above self-reflection and work on perfecting these new routines.

If you keep going tweaking your routines, you will be regularly improving your them until they are perfect.

Your commitment to creating and perfecting routines, will actually become a routine itself!

The power of routine is a powerful force that only gets more powerful as you fully acknowledge and embrace it. Anyone who follows these steps is doing both.

Is It Time For Change?

For this section, honesty is paramount. Take the quiz below and try to be as honest as possible. Don't overthink the questions.

Answer **yes** or **no** quickly and definitively for the most accurate results (results on next page).

You can write your answers down here, or just keep a rough tally in your head.

1. Do you sense that things in your life just aren't right?

2. Do you feel like you are stuck in a routine?

3. Are you ignoring your mental or physical health?

4. Do you often get jealous of other people?

5. Do you start yearning for the weekend as soon as it is over?

6. Do you often get lost in thoughts of the past?

7. Do you find it tough to get up in the morning?

8. Do you suffer from bouts of unhappiness?

9. Are you indifferent to your surroundings & circumstances?

10. Does everyone or everything seem to annoy you?

Quiz Results:

0 Yes Answers: You seem to be doing well! You seem to be on track, and maybe you don't need to make any serious changes right now.

1 Yes Answer: You also seem to be doing pretty well. It might not seem like much, but if you answered yes to even one question, you should still work through this book.

2-5 Yes Answers: You might not need a complete overhaul, but there is something in your life that you are itching to change. Work through this book to see if you can narrow down what it is.

5+ Yes Answers: You likely have something that you need to change in your life, and it might even be a few things. Working through this book will be a massive help to you, please do not hesitate.

What Do I Need to Change?

If you are reading this, you have realized that you need to change something in your life. You might even already know what it is. I think it's important to work through this exercise regardless. You might stumble across other changes you need to make, maybe things you haven't even thought of yet.

Brainstorming Change

The first thing we are going to have you do is brainstorm the things in your life you'd like to change. No wrong answers here, and no change is "too small".

THINGS I WOULD LIKE TO CHANGE

What Would Others Change About You

This is a very similar exercise as before, but the way it is framed forces your mind to think a little differently. Instead of thinking about the things you want to change, think about what other people would want you to change.

Focus solely on the people that matter to you. Think about people like your colleagues, boss, family, friends, roommates, and/or partner.

Pro Tip: *Ask these people!*

Example: My girlfriend would like me to be more open with my feelings.

THINGS OTHER PEOPLE WOULD CHANGE ABOUT ME

Prioritizing Change

If you worked through the above two exercises you should have quite a few changes you'd like to make in your life.

Don't worry if you haven't listed many because sometimes it's apparent what you need to change. That said, take all the time you need for the above exercises. Sometimes walking away from the brainstorming and coming back another day will help you think of more ideas.

***

Now take your lists from last exercise and highlight 3-5 changes that you would like to change the most. Just doodle a star beside them, or go ahead and list them here:

1.

2.

3.

4.

5.

This doesn't mean we will forget about our other changes; it just helps us narrow down what to focus on first.

Out of the above list, choose one change to make – and work through the **Time to Change Worksheets** on the following pages. We include 5 of these worksheets but you can use any type of journal to do more.

Time To Change

The following pages include five worksheets that you can use to create a plan of action for your each of the changes you want to make.

Change #1

_____

_____

The Change Matrix

How Will This Change Help Me?	Who Am I Making This Change For?
Who Can Help Me With This Change?	What Happens If I Don't Make This Change?

Five Steps You Can Take to Make Your Change

1.

2.

3.

4.

5.

One Step You Can Take Right Now!

_____

_____

Track Your Change

Track your changes for 3 weeks, every day that you work towards change, check off a box below. Try to get all 21 days in a row!

Change #2

_____

_____

The Change Matrix

How Will This Change Help Me?	Who Am I Making This Change For?
Who Can Help Me With This Change?	What Happens If I Don't Make This Change?

Five Steps You Can Take to Make Your Change

1.

2.

3.

4.

5.

One Step You Can Take Right Now!

_____

_____

Track Your Change

Track your changes for 3 weeks, every day that you work towards change, check off a box below. Try to get all 21 days in a row!

Change #3

_____

_____

The Change Matrix

How Will This Change Help Me?	Who Am I Making This Change For?
Who Can Help Me With This Change?	What Happens If I Don't Make This Change?

Five Steps You Can Take to Make Your Change

1.

2.

3.

4.

5.

One Step You Can Take Right Now!

_____

_____

Track Your Change

Track your changes for 3 weeks, every day that you work towards change, check off a box below. Try to get all 21 days in a row!

Change #4

_____

_____

The Change Matrix

How Will This Change Help Me?	**Who Am I Making This Change For?**
Who Can Help Me With This Change?	**What Happens If I Don't Make This Change?**

Five Steps You Can Take to Make Your Change

1.

2.

3.

4.

5.

One Step You Can Take Right Now!

_____

_____

Track Your Change

Track your changes for 3 weeks, every day that you work towards change, check off a box below. Try to get all 21 days in a row!

Change #5

_____

_____

The Change Matrix

How Will This Change Help Me?	Who Am I Making This Change For?
Who Can Help Me With This Change?	**What Happens If I Don't Make This Change?**

Five Steps You Can Take to Make Your Change

1.

2.

3.

4.

5.

One Step You Can Take Right Now!

_____

_____

Track Your Change

Track your changes for 3 weeks, every day that you work towards change, check off a box below. Try to get all 21 days in a row!

Conclusion

One of life's truths: Change is inevitable.

If you agree with that, then you are wasting your energy fighting it. It is time you not only accept change in your life – you embrace it.

Change is new life. Change is fresh starts. Change is progress.

It is also scary. Hopefully this workbook gives you some inspiration to make positive change in your life.

If you worked through this book already, you know:

- If it's time for a change
- What you want to change
- What others want you to change
- The change you want to make first
- How to make that change

All that is left to do is **pivot** and get started!

To all the new and exciting changes in your life, we wish you the best.

www.ingramcontent.com/pod-product-compliance
Lightning Source LLC
Chambersburg PA
CBHW081549040426
42448CB00015B/3262